The Power Play Of Positivity: Unleashing Success in Hockey Leadership

Jonathan Paul, Esq., MBA

D1516842

Dear Hockey Leader,

As a reader of this book, we are thrilled to offer you an exclusive opportunity to participate in our FREE, comprehensive three-module program, specifically tailored for hockey leaders like you.

Jonathan Paul, a highly accomplished professional with an impressive educational background and a deep passion for hockey, has designed this program to empower you to excel in your role and drive lasting change in the sport.

Simply go to **www.lawyer.hockey** and click on "Hockey Leadership Program" on top menu or scan the QR code on this page.

Here's a sneak peek of what you can expect:

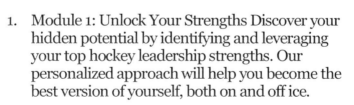

SCAN ME

1. Module 1: Unlock Your Strengths Discover your hidden potential by identifying and leveraging your top hockey leadership strengths. Our personalized approach will help you become the best version of yourself, both on and off ice.

2. Module 2: Part 1 - Master Emotional and Social Intelligence (ESI) Enhance your ability to connect with others, understand their emotions, and navigate complex social dynamics. This module will sharpen your ESI skills as a hockey leader, enabling you to foster better team collaboration, communication, and performance.

Part 2 - Champion Diversity, Equity, and Inclusion (DEI) Learn how to create an inclusive environment that values and respects diverse perspectives. By promoting DEI, you can contribute to a stronger, more unified hockey community that thrives on the ice and beyond.

3. Module 3: The Three-Dimensional Leadership Framework Discover the power of the Vision, Alignment, and Execution framework to lead your team to success. This transformative approach will equip you with the tools to set ambitious goals, inspire your team, and achieve remarkable results.

Don't miss this unique opportunity to learn from the best and transform your leadership abilities. Always feel free to reach out personally to chat; my email is **jp@elitehockeyleadership.com**

We will see you around the rinks

Jonathan

THE POWER OF POSITIVE LEADERSHIP: SHAPING SUCCESS IN THE WORLD OF HOCKEY

In the fast-paced, high-stakes world of hockey, success is often measured by goals scored, games won, and championships secured. Yet, at the heart of every triumphant team is a leader whose influence goes beyond the scoreboard.

Positive leadership, an approach that focuses on cultivating a supportive, empowering environment, can be the driving force behind a team's success both on and off ice. In this chapter, we'll explore the key tenets of positive leadership and how they can shape the world of hockey, fostering growth, resilience, and a winning mindset in players and coaches alike.

Encouraging a Growth Mindset

Positive leadership in hockey begins with fostering a growth mindset among players and coaching staff. By emphasizing the importance of effort, learning, and self-improvement, leaders can help their teams embrace challenges and view setbacks as opportunities to grow. This mindset not only builds resilience but also nurtures an environment where players are motivated to push themselves and continually strive for excellence.

Building Trust and Open Communication

Trust and open communication are the cornerstones of positive leadership. Hockey leaders who cultivate an environment where players feel comfortable expressing their thoughts, concerns, and ideas foster a strong sense of unity and camaraderie. This trust-based culture not only promotes accountability but also enables players to learn from one another and collaborate effectively, ultimately leading to better decision making and performance on the ice.

Empowering Players

Empowering players is a critical aspect of positive leadership in hockey. By entrusting individuals with responsibilities and providing them with the tools and support to succeed, leaders can inspire confidence, autonomy, and ownership among their team members. This empowerment can result in increased motivation, engagement, and a collective drive to achieve shared goals.

Celebrating Small Victories and Recognizing Effort

In the world of hockey, where the focus often lies on the final score, positive leaders understand the value of celebrating small victories and recognizing effort. Acknowledging individual and team accomplishments, no matter how minor, can boost morale and foster a sense of pride and belonging. By emphasizing the importance of effort and incremental progress, positive leaders can inspire their teams to maintain a high level of dedication and commitment to their goals.

Promoting a Healthy Team Culture

A healthy team culture is essential to the success of any hockey organization. Positive leaders prioritize the well-being of their players, ensuring that physical, mental, and emotional health are valued and supported. By fostering a culture of respect, inclusion, and support, leaders can create an environment where players feel valued and empowered to reach their full potential both on and off the ice.

Leading by Example

Positive leadership in hockey requires leaders to model the behaviors, attitudes, and values they wish to see in their players. By demonstrating qualities like dedication, resilience, and humility, leaders can set the tone for their teams and inspire those around them to follow suit. As role models, leaders have a unique opportunity to influence the development and growth of their players, shaping not only their performance on the ice but also their character and personal growth.

Key Takeaway

Positive leadership has the power to transform the world of hockey, fostering success that transcends the win-loss column. By encouraging a growth mindset, building trust and open communication, empowering players, celebrating small victories, promoting a healthy team culture, and leading by example, hockey leaders can create an environment where players thrive both on and off the ice.

The impact of positive leadership extends far beyond the rink, shaping the lives of athletes and coaches alike and inspiring a new generation of leaders dedicated to nurturing the true spirit of the game.

UNRAVELING HOCKEY CULTURE: HISTORICAL CONTEXT, CURRENT TRENDS, AND CHALLENGES IN POSITIVE LEADERSHIP

Hockey, a sport that combines speed, skill, and toughness, has captivated millions of fans worldwide since its emergence in the late 19th century. The culture surrounding this sport has evolved significantly over time, but its core principles of teamwork, camaraderie, and resilience have remained steadfast.

In this chapter, we delve into the historical context of hockey culture, examine current trends and challenges, and explore the role of positive leadership in shaping the future of this beloved sport.

Historical Context: The Emergence of Hockey Culture

The early years of hockey were marked by a sense of camaraderie among players, who often hailed from small, close-knit communities. This sense of unity and support was a defining characteristic of the sport, manifested in the on-ice battles and off-ice friendships that were integral to its charm.

Hockey's expansion over the years saw it develop into a multi-faceted cultural phenomenon that transcended mere sport, becoming a symbol of national pride and a celebration of regional identities.

Hockey's cultural significance was further solidified through its connection to the military, as the sport was often used to boost morale during times of conflict. This military association reinforced hockey's image as a sport that prized strength, grit, and determination, qualities that remain central to its identity today.

Current Trends: The Evolving Face of Hockey Culture

In recent years, hockey culture has witnessed a series of significant changes, both on and off the ice. The sport has become increasingly diverse, with a growing number of players from various ethnic and cultural backgrounds joining the ranks of professional leagues. This has led to a more inclusive and representative hockey community, one that better reflects the sport's global fan base.

Another significant trend is the increased focus on player safety, as the long-term consequences of injuries and the dangers of playing through pain have become more widely acknowledged. This has led to an emphasis on concussion protocols, as well as efforts to reduce the prevalence of fighting and dangerous hits in the game.

Challenges: Addressing Issues in Hockey Culture

Despite these positive developments, hockey culture still faces several challenges. Instances of racism, sexism, and homophobia have marred the sport, highlighting the need for a more inclusive and respectful environment. Additionally, the hyper-competitive nature of hockey can sometimes foster a toxic "win-at-all-costs" mentality that undermines the values of sportsmanship and fair play.

Positive Leadership: Shaping the Future of Hockey

To address these challenges and ensure a brighter future for hockey, positive leadership plays a crucial role. This type of leadership is characterized by the following principles:

1. Emphasizing Character Development:
Positive leaders prioritize the development of strong character traits, such as integrity, humility, and empathy, in players. By instilling these values,

leaders can create a more inclusive and respectful hockey culture.

2. Promoting Diversity and Inclusion: Positive leaders actively seek to break down barriers and create opportunities for individuals from all backgrounds to participate in and enjoy the sport.

3. Encouraging Mental and Physical Wellbeing: By fostering a culture that values mental and physical health, positive leaders
can help players to prioritize their wellbeing and make more informed decisions about their participation in the sport.

4. Championing Sportsmanship and Fair Play: Positive leaders emphasize the importance of sportsmanship, both on and off the ice, and strive to create an environment where players can compete with integrity and respect.

The evolution of hockey culture has been marked by both progress and challenges. By understanding its historical context and current trends, we can better appreciate the importance of positive leadership in shaping the sport's future.

EMBRACING POSITIVE LEADERSHIP: THE HOCKEY COACH'S GUIDE TO INSPIRING SUCCESS AND BUILDING CHARACTER

The role of a hockey coach extends far beyond developing players' skills and implementing game strategies. A truly successful coach is a positive leader who fosters an environment that promotes personal growth, inclusivity, and a love for the game.

In this chapter, we will explore the various facets of positive leadership and provide practical guidance for hockey coaches seeking to embody these principles.

Building Trust and Strong Relationships

At the core of positive leadership is the ability to build trust and forge strong relationships with players.

Communicate openly and honestly:

Clear, honest communication helps players understand their roles and responsibilities, builds trust, and fosters a supportive team environment.

Show genuine care and concern:

Take the time to understand your players' needs and challenges, both on and off the ice. Show empathy and offer support when they face difficulties.

Recognize and celebrate individual achievements: Acknowledge the hard work and accomplishments of each player, reinforcing their value to the team.

Emphasizing Character Development

A positive leader places a strong emphasis on character development, instilling values that extend beyond the hockey rink: Teach and model integrity: Encourage players to be honest, accountable, and to treat others with respect.

Foster humility and teamwork

Encourage players to recognize the importance of every team member and promote a selfless, team-first mentality.

Cultivate empathy

Help players understand and appreciate the perspectives and feelings of their teammates, opponents, and officials.

Promoting Diversity and Inclusion

As the face of hockey becomes more diverse, it is crucial for positive leaders to create an inclusive environment.

Encourage open dialogue:

Provide opportunities for players to discuss their experiences, perspectives, and ideas, fostering understanding and respect for individual differences.

Challenge biases and stereotypes:

Confront and address discriminatory language or behavior and educate players about the importance of equality and inclusivity.

Actively recruit and support diverse players. Seek out players from various backgrounds and ensure they have equal opportunities to succeed.

Fostering Mental and Physical Well-being

Positive leaders recognize the importance of mental and physical well-being in the development of successful players.

Encourage self-care and healthy habits

Teach players the importance of proper nutrition, hydration, sleep, and mental health care. Provide support for injury prevention and recovery:

Implement injury prevention strategies, and ensure injured players receive appropriate care and support for a safe return to play.

Create a safe, supportive environment
Foster a team culture that allows players to express their feelings, concerns, and vulnerabilities without fear of judgment.

Championing Sportsmanship and Fair Play
A commitment to sportsmanship and fair play is central to positive leadership: Set clear expectations: Establish and communicate team values and expectations related to sportsmanship and fair play.

Model appropriate behavior
Demonstrate respect for opponents, officials, and the game itself, and hold yourself accountable for your actions.

<u>Encourage players to take responsibility</u>

Empower players to recognize their own actions and take responsibility for their behavior on and off the ice.

Positive leadership in hockey is a transformative force, capable of shaping not only individual players but also the wider culture of the sport.

By embracing the principles of positive leadership and implementing the strategies outlined in this chapter, hockey coaches can create an environment that nurtures personal growth, fosters inclusivity, and cultivates a lifelong love for the game.

Here are three examples of coaches outside of the NHL using positive leadership to create success:

1. Valeri Bragin and the Russian Junior National Team: Valeri Bragin, a highly successful coach in international junior hockey, has used positive leadership to create success with the Russian Junior National Team. Bragin emphasizes teamwork,

discipline, and a strong work ethic, fostering a supportive and goal-oriented environment for his players.

Under his guidance, the Russian Junior National Team has experienced significant success at the IIHF World Junior Championships, winning multiple medals, including gold in 2011 and 2020. Bragin's positive leadership approach has not only led to success on the ice but has also helped develop many talented players who have gone on to have successful careers in the NHL and other professional leagues.

2. Shannon Miller and the Canadian Women's National Team: Shannon Miller, a pioneer in women's hockey coaching, utilized positive leadership to create success with the Canadian Women's National Team. As the head coach from 1997 to 2000, Miller focused on empowering her players, fostering a strong sense of team unity, and promoting hard work and commitment.

Under Miller's leadership, the Canadian Women's National Team won several international tournaments, including the 1997 and 2000 IIHF Women's World Championships and a silver medal at the 1998 Winter Olympics. Miller's positive leadership approach not only led to success on the ice but also helped to pave the way for future generations of women's hockey players and coaches.

3. Bengt-Åke Gustafsson and the Swedish National Team: Bengt-Åke Gustafsson, a former NHL player and accomplished international coach, has used positive leadership to create success with the Swedish National Team. As the head coach from 2005 to 2010, Gustafsson prioritized building a cohesive team culture that emphasized skill, creativity, and collective responsibility. Under his guidance, the Swedish National Team experienced significant success, including winning the gold medal at the 2006 Winter Olympics in Turin. Gustafsson's positive leadership approach not only led to on-ice success but also helped to inspire and develop many talented Swedish players who have

gone onto make significant contributions to the sport at the highest levels.

EMBODYING POSITIVE LEADERSHIP: A GUIDE FOR INDIVIDUAL HOCKEY PLAYERS

While the coach plays a critical role in creating a positive team environment, individual players also play a significant part in team dynamics and success. As a hockey player, you can contribute to building a supportive and inclusive atmosphere by embodying the principles of positive leadership. In this chapter, we will explore the different aspects of positive leadership from the perspective of an individual player and provide practical advice on how to be a positive leader within your team.

One effective way to promote positive leadership is to lead by example and demonstrate the qualities you want to see in your teammates. This includes displaying a strong work ethic, showing dedication and commitment to self-improvement during practices, games, and off-ice training. It also involves demonstrating respect and sportsmanship towards opponents, officials, and teammates and always playing within the rules of the game. Additionally, maintaining a positive attitude and encouraging your teammates, even in challenging situations, is crucial.

Fostering trust and building strong relationships with your teammates is another critical aspect of positive leadership. You can do this by being open and approachable, encouraging open communication and actively listening to your teammates' thoughts, feelings, and concerns.

Offering support and encouragement to your teammates in times of need, providing words of encouragement, guidance, or a helping hand can also build trust. Celebrating the achievements of others is also an essential component of positive leadership.

To foster a positive team environment, it's important to acknowledge and appreciate your teammates' accomplishments and recognize the collective effort that contributes to the team's success.

As a positive leader, you can also help instill and reinforce important values and character traits within your team. These include encouraging accountability and integrity, fostering a team-first mentality that prioritizes the success and well-being of the team over individual accomplishments, and showing empathy and understanding towards your teammates.

Embracing diversity and creating an inclusive environment is also crucial for a team's success and growth. This involves standing against discrimination and actively challenging prejudiced language, attitudes, or behavior within the team environment. You can also encourage open dialogue about diversity and inclusivity and advocate for equal opportunities, supporting the inclusion and development of teammates from all backgrounds and skill levels.

Prioritizing mental and physical well-being for both you and your teammates is also a crucial aspect of positive leadership. This involves practicing self-care by maintaining healthy habits, seeking support when needed, and setting appropriate boundaries.

You can also encourage your teammates to take care of their mental and physical health and offer support when they face challenges. Additionally, fostering a safe, supportive environment that encourages open communication, vulnerability, and mutual support can contribute to a positive team culture.

As an individual player, you have the power to positively influence your team's culture through leadership. By embracing the principles outlined in this chapter, you can help create an environment that fosters personal growth, inclusivity, and a love for the game. By doing so, you not only enhance your own hockey experience but also contribute to the success and well-being of your teammates and the sport.

Positive leadership is a crucial element of a successful team. Here are three examples of players who have used positive leadership to inspire their teams to greatness:

1. Wayne Gretzky - Wayne Gretzky is widely regarded as the greatest hockey player of all time, and he was also an exceptional leader during his time as captain of the Edmonton Oilers and later the Los Angeles Kings. Gretzky led by example, demonstrating an incredible work ethic, sportsmanship, and dedication to the team's success. As a captain, he fostered a positive environment that encouraged his teammates to perform at their best and support each other, both on and off the ice. Under Gretzky's leadership, the Oilers won four Stanley Cup championships, in 1984, 1985, 1987, and 1988.

2. Steve Yzerman - Steve Yzerman served as the captain of the Detroit Red Wings for 19 seasons, making him one of the longest-serving captains in NHL history. Yzerman's leadership style was characterized by his humility, commitment, and ability to inspire and motivate his teammates. His emphasis on teamwork, sportsmanship, and personal growth contributed to a positive team culture that led to the Red Wings' considerable success during his tenure, including three Stanley Cup championships in 1997, 1998, and 2002.

3. Jonathan Toews - Jonathan Toews has been the captain of the Chicago Blackhawks since 2008 and has been an advocate of positive leadership throughout his career. Known for his strong work ethic, determination, and ability to remain calm under pressure, Toews has been instrumental in building a winning

culture within the Blackhawks organization. He has fostered an environment that values teamwork, accountability, and personal development, leading the team to three Stanley Cup championships in 2010, 2013, and 2015. Toews' leadership has also extended beyond the rink, as he actively participates in community and charitable initiatives, setting an example for his teammates and the wider hockey community.

These three players exemplify the power of positive leadership and its impact on a team's success. By leading by example, fostering a positive team culture, and prioritizing personal growth and development, they have inspired their teammates to perform at their best and achieve greatness. Their legacies as exceptional leaders serve as an inspiration for future generations of hockey players to follow in their footsteps.

STEERING THE SHIP: THE ROLE OF GENERAL MANAGERS AND FRONT OFFICE STAFF IN POSITIVE LEADERSHIP

General managers and front office staff in hockey organizations play a crucial role in creating and maintaining a positive team culture. They are responsible for establishing a clear vision and core values that guide the organization's direction, as well as assembling a team of coaches, support staff, and players who embody these principles.

One important aspect of positive leadership for general managers is prioritizing character in talent evaluation. This means looking beyond a player's on-ice abilities and considering their work ethic, commitment to the team's values, and overall character when scouting and acquiring players. By building a roster with not only skill, but also strong character, GMs can create a team that is not only successful on the ice but also serves as a positive influence within the community.

Another key responsibility of general managers and front office staff is fostering collaboration and communication among the leadership team. By promoting an environment of open dialogue and a unified approach to decision-making, they can create a team culture that prioritizes teamwork, accountability, and mutual support.

Engaging with the community and fans is another important aspect of positive leadership for GMs and front office staff. By developing community outreach initiatives and encouraging player involvement, they can foster positive relationships with fans and local organizations, while also reinforcing the team's values and role within the community.

Overall, embracing positive leadership principles is crucial for the long-term success and growth of a hockey organization. By prioritizing character, collaboration, and community engagement, GMs and front office staff can create an environment that fosters personal growth, inclusivity, and success both on and off the ice.

Here are some recent examples:

1. Don Sweeney and the Boston Bruins: Don Sweeney has been the general manager of the Boston Bruins since 2015 and has prioritized a positive leadership approach in his role. Sweeney has emphasized the importance of communication and collaboration within the team, working closely with the coaching staff and players to create a culture of teamwork and mutual support. He has also emphasized the importance of developing and nurturing talent within the organization, investing in player development programs and initiatives to help players reach their full potential.

Under Sweeney's leadership, the Bruins have continued to be a competitive team in the league, making it to the playoffs in each of the past six seasons.

2. Lou Lamoriello is known for his dedication to positive leadership throughout his successful career as an NHL general manager. He has managed several teams, including the New Jersey Devils, Toronto Maple Leafs, and currently, the New York Islanders. Lamoriello instills a strong work ethic, discipline, and a team-first mentality in the organizations he manages, creating a positive environment that fosters growth and development. His emphasis on character and commitment has contributed to his teams' consistent success, including three Stanley Cup championships with the Devils.

3. Ken Holland is a strong advocate of positive leadership in his role as the current general manager of the Edmonton Oilers and

formerly of the Detroit Red Wings. During his time with the Red Wings, Holland prioritized drafting and developing players with strong character and a commitment to the team's success. His focus on building a positive culture within the organization contributed to the Red Wings' sustained success, including four Stanley Cup championships. Holland continues to emphasize positive leadership in his role with the Oilers, fostering an environment of growth, collaboration, and accountability.

4. Steve Yzerman, a legendary NHL player and current general manager, emphasizes positive leadership principles in the teams he manages. As the general manager of the Tampa Bay Lightning from 2010 to 2018, Yzerman focused on building a strong, supportive culture within the organization, which led to consistent success on the ice. In his current role as general manager of the Detroit Red Wings, Yzerman continues to

prioritize character, teamwork, and personal growth, aiming to recreate the winning culture he experienced both as a player and a manager. Yzerman's emphasis on positive leadership has contributed to his team's success both on and off the ice.

THE IMPACT OF OWNERSHIP: FOSTERING POSITIVE LEADERSHIP FROM THE TOP

In the world of professional hockey, team owners have a significant role in shaping the culture and direction of their organizations. As the ultimate decision-makers, they have a unique opportunity to create an environment that fosters positive leadership and sets the stage for long-term success both on and off ice.

Establishing the Foundation for Positive Leadership

Team owners have a profound influence on the organization's culture, and they can inspire a ripple effect throughout the entire organization by establishing a solid foundation for positive leadership. Here are some ways team owners can create that foundation:

Clearly define and communicate your vision: Outline your organization's core values and principles, emphasizing the importance of character development, inclusivity, and sportsmanship. Communicate this vision to your general manager, front office staff, coaches, and players, ensuring that everyone understands and is committed to these guiding principles.

Be a role model for positive leadership: Embody the values and principles you wish to see within your organization. Demonstrate integrity, humility, and empathy in your decision-making and interactions, setting a strong example for others to follow.

Foster a culture of collaboration and communication: Encourage open dialogue and collaboration among all members of the organization, promoting a unified approach to decision-making and problem-solving.

Empowering the Right People

One of the most significant decisions team owners will make is the selection of their general manager and front office staff. These individuals play a critical role in implementing the owner's vision and fostering positive leadership within the organization. Here are some ways team owners can empower the right people:

Hire leaders with strong character and a track record of success: Seek out general managers and front office staff who not only have experience and expertise in their respective roles but also demonstrate strong character traits, such as integrity, humility, and empathy.

Provide support and resources: Ensure that your general manager and front office staff have the necessary resources and support to be effective in their roles. This includes providing opportunities for professional development, access to cutting-edge technology, and a supportive working environment.

Establish clear expectations and accountability: Communicate your expectations for performance, adherence to the organization's values, and commitment to positive leadership. Hold your general manager and front office staff accountable for their actions and decisions, reinforcing the importance of leading by example.

Investing in the Future

Team owners can demonstrate their commitment to positive leadership by investing in the future of the organization and the sport. Here are some ways team owners can invest in the future:

Support player development and well-being: Allocate resources to ensure that players have access to top-notch facilities, coaching, and support staff, as well as resources for their physical, mental, and emotional well-being.

Promote diversity and inclusivity: Champion initiatives that promote diversity and inclusivity within the organization, including hiring practices, player development programs, and community outreach efforts.

Engage with youth and grassroots hockey: Invest in programs that support youth and grassroots hockey, fostering a love for the sport and creating opportunities for future generations to participate and excel.

Building Strong Connections with the Community and Fans

Positive leadership extends beyond the organization and into the broader community. Here are some ways team owners can build strong connections with the community and fans:

Engage with fans and the community: Be visible and accessible to fans and the local community, demonstrating your commitment to their support and involvement.

Support community initiatives and charitable efforts: Allocate resources and time to support local charities, community programs, and events that align with your organization's values and vision.

Foster a positive fan experience: Strive to create a welcoming, inclusive, and enjoyable environment for fans attending games and engaging with your organization through various platforms.

When it comes to the NHL, positive leadership is a key component of success both on and off the ice. Here are three examples of NHL owners who have used positive leadership to build winning teams:

Ed Snider and the Philadelphia Flyers: Ed Snider, the late founder and longtime owner of the Philadelphia Flyers, was known for his unwavering dedication to his team and its players. He created a family-like atmosphere within the organization, taking a hands-on approach in supporting his players and staff, and fostering a culture of loyalty and success. Under his ownership, the Flyers won two Stanley Cups and consistently maintained a competitive and passionate team. Beyond the rink, Snider founded the Ed Snider Youth Hockey Foundation, which provides opportunities for underprivileged youth to participate in hockey and develop important life skills.

Mike Ilitch and the Detroit Red Wings: Mike Ilitch, the late owner of the Detroit Red Wings, played a significant role in revitalizing the team and creating a positive culture that led to sustained success. Ilitch was committed to investing in the team's success, both financially and emotionally, and this was instrumental in building a strong foundation for the Red Wings. Under his ownership, the team won four Stanley Cup championships and made the playoffs for 25 consecutive seasons. Ilitch was known for his dedication to the players, staff, and fans, and he played an active role in supporting the Detroit community through various philanthropic endeavors.

Mario Lemieux and the Pittsburgh Penguins: Mario Lemieux, the former NHL player and current owner of the Pittsburgh Penguins, has played a pivotal role in the team's success by fostering a positive leadership culture. Lemieux's unique perspective as a former player has allowed him to create an environment focused on player well-being, support, and development. His commitment to building a winning culture and investing in the organization's future has resulted in three Stanley Cup championships under his ownership. Additionally, Lemieux has been an advocate for community involvement and philanthropy, founding the Mario Lemieux Foundation, which supports cancer research and patient care initiatives.

Jeff Vinik and the Tampa Bay Lightning: Jeff Vinik, the owner of the Tampa Bay Lightning, has been praised for his commitment to positive leadership and community involvement. Vinik's ownership has been marked by a focus on developing a winning team culture that is also a positive force in the community. He has invested in player development, built state-of-the-art facilities, and created a supportive working environment for his staff. Under his ownership, the Lightning has won two Stanley Cup championships and has been active in supporting various community initiatives, such as the Lightning Community Heroes program and the Vinik Sports Group's community development efforts.

ADVOCATES OF POSITIVE LEADERSHIP: THE ROLE OF NHLPA AGENTS IN SHAPING PLAYER EXPERIENCES

The role of NHLPA agents in the lives and careers of professional hockey players is critical. These agents not only act as advocates but also offer guidance and support in various aspects of a player's life, both on and off ice. To be effective in their roles and to foster positive leadership, NHLPA agents must focus on building strong relationships, maintaining open communication, and demonstrating honesty and transparency.

One way to foster trust and open communication is to develop genuine, long-lasting relationships with clients. NHLPA agents can show genuine interest in their clients' lives, goals, and well-being.

Encouraging open dialogue and actively listening to their clients' concerns, aspirations, and feedback can help build strong relationships. Demonstrating honesty and transparency in all aspects of their work is essential for NHLPA agents to maintain the trust of their clients.

NHLPA agents can provide comprehensive support and guidance to their clients in various aspects of their lives. They can offer expert advice during contract negotiations, career guidance that aligns with their clients' goals and values, and support personal development and mentorship. Providing resources and guidance to help clients make informed financial decisions and prepare for life after hockey is crucial.

Advocating for player welfare and mental health is a key aspect of positive leadership. NHLPA agents should encourage their clients to maintain a healthy work-life balance and facilitate access to mental health resources and support as needed. They should also actively advocate for their clients in addressing any concerns or challenges they may face within their teams or the league.

Encouraging community involvement and personal values is another way NHLPA agents can promote positive leadership. They can help their clients find opportunities to give back to their communities, pursue their personal interests and values outside of hockey, and reinforce the importance of sportsmanship, respect, and fair play in their interactions with others.

Here are five examples of agents practicing positive leadership:

Pat Brisson: Pat Brisson is a prominent NHLPA agent who represents several top NHL players, including Sidney Crosby and Patrick Kane. Brisson has been recognized for his commitment to player advocacy and positive leadership. He emphasizes building strong relationships with his clients, providing comprehensive support and guidance, and promoting player welfare and mental health.

Don Meehan: Don Meehan is a veteran NHLPA agent who has represented NHL players for over 40 years. Meehan is known for his integrity, professionalism, and commitment to positive leadership. He emphasizes the importance of building trust and open communication with his clients, providing expert advice and guidance, and advocating for player welfare and mental health.

Kurt Overhardt: Kurt Overhardt is a well-respected NHLPA agent who represents several high-profile NHL players, including Johnny Gaudreau and Seth Jones. Overhardt is known for his commitment to building strong relationships with his clients, providing comprehensive support and guidance, and advocating for player welfare and mental health.

Craig Oster: Craig Oster is a former NHL player who is now a prominent NHLPA agent, representing several NHL players, including Max Pacioretty and T.J. Oshie. Oster is committed to promoting positive leadership and advocating for players' welfare and mental health. He emphasizes the importance of building strong relationships with his clients and providing comprehensive support and guidance.

Allan Walsh: Allan Walsh is a veteran NHLPA agent who has represented NHL players for over 20 years. Walsh is committed to promoting positive leadership and advocating for player welfare and mental health. He emphasizes building trust and open communication with his clients, providing expert advice and guidance, and advocating for their well-being both on and off the ice.

CULTIVATING SUCCESS: BUILDING A POSITIVE TEAM CULTURE IN THE WORLD OF HOCKEY

A positive team culture is the backbone of successful hockey teams. In this chapter, we will explore the various aspects of positive leadership and how it contributes to building a thriving team culture in the hockey world. We will discuss the key attributes of positive leadership, strategies for fostering a positive environment, and the benefits that result from implementing these practices.

I. The Importance of Positive Leadership

Positive leadership is essential in guiding a hockey team towards success. The most successful teams have strong leaders who promote a positive atmosphere, build strong relationships, and inspire their teammates to achieve their full potential. A positive leader is someone who:

Develops a shared vision: A clear and inspiring vision unites the team and provides a sense of purpose, direction, and motivation.
Models the desired behavior: A leader's actions set the tone for the team. By modeling the desired behavior, they create a standard for others to follow.

Encourages open communication: Positive leaders facilitate open and honest communication, fostering trust and collaboration among team members.

Empowers team members: They give their teammates the tools, resources, and autonomy to take ownership of their roles, promoting personal growth and development.

Recognizes and appreciates efforts: Acknowledging and rewarding the hard work and achievements of team members strengthens morale and motivation.

II. Strategies for Fostering a Positive Team Culture

To create a positive team culture, leaders must implement strategies that promote cohesion, mutual respect, and personal growth. Here are some approaches that can be employed:

Establish clear goals and expectations: Defining specific, measurable, achievable, relevant, and time-bound (SMART) goals sets a clear path to success.

Encourage team bonding: Off-ice activities, such as team dinners or community service events, help build camaraderie and trust among teammates.

Provide constructive feedback: Providing honest, specific, and actionable feedback helps team members grow and improve.

Promote a growth mindset: Encouraging players to embrace challenges and view setbacks as opportunities for learning fosters resilience and adaptability.

Develop a supportive environment: Encourage teammates to support each other, both on and off the ice, and to celebrate each other's accomplishments.

III. The Benefits of a Positive Team Culture

A positive team culture brings numerous benefits to both individual players and the team, such as:

Improved performance: A positive environment fosters motivation, focus, and determination, leading to enhanced individual and team performance.

Enhanced resilience: Teams with a positive culture are better equipped to handle setbacks, learn from mistakes, and bounce back stronger.

Greater player satisfaction: Players who feel supported, valued, and respected are more likely to enjoy their hockey experience and remain committed to the team.

Stronger team cohesion: When team members trust and respect each other, they are more likely to work together effectively and collaborate towards a shared goal.

Attracting top talent: A positive team culture is an asset that attracts skilled players who want to be part of a winning and supportive environment.

Conclusion

Cultivating success in the world of hockey requires a strong foundation built on positive leadership and a supportive team culture. By employing effective strategies and fostering an environment that promotes personal growth, mutual respect, and open communication, leaders can guide their teams to new heights of achievement. In doing so, they will create a legacy of success that extends beyond the ice, shaping the lives of players and the hockey community for years to come.

DEVELOPING A TEAM MISSION AND VISION IN HOCKEY

Establishing a clear mission and vision is vital for any hockey team aiming for success. A well-defined mission and vision provide direction, purpose, and a sense of unity among team members.

In this chapter, we will delve into the importance of having a mission and vision for hockey teams, the process of creating them, and the methods for effectively communicating and implementing these guiding principles.

I. The Importance of a Team Mission and Vision in Hockey

A team mission and vision serve as the foundation of a strong and unified hockey team. They offer the following benefits:

Direction: A clear mission and vision provide a roadmap for the team's aspirations, guiding players and coaches in their decision-making processes.

Purpose: They instill a sense of purpose and shared goals, motivating team members to strive for excellence and contribute to the team's success.

Unity: A common mission and vision unify players from diverse backgrounds, fostering cohesion and collaboration.

Accountability: They establish a framework for measuring progress and holding team members accountable for their performance.

Identity: A well-articulated mission and vision help define the team's identity and create a unique brand that distinguishes the team from others.

II. Creating a Team Mission and Vision

Developing a mission and vision requires a collaborative approach that involves input from key stakeholders, including coaches, team leaders, and players. The process should follow these steps:

Assess the current situation: Evaluate the team's strengths, weaknesses, opportunities, and threats (SWOT analysis) to identify areas for improvement and potential goals.

Identify core values: Determine the values that will guide the team's actions and decisions, such as teamwork, integrity, dedication, and respect.

Establish a vision: Develop a long-term vision for the team that outlines the desired future state. The vision should be inspiring, ambitious, and aligned with the team's core values.

Define a mission: Craft a mission statement that succinctly describes the team's purpose and its commitment to achieving its vision. The mission should be clear, concise, and actionable.

Set short- and long-term goals: Establish specific, measurable, achievable, relevant, and time-bound (SMART) goals that support the team's mission and vision.

III. Communicating the Team Mission and Vision

For a mission and vision to have a meaningful impact, they must be effectively communicated and reinforced throughout the team. Here are some strategies for doing so:

Present the mission and vision to the team: Organize a team meeting or event to introduce the mission and vision, explaining their significance and the process of creating them.

Display the mission and vision: Place visual reminders of the mission and vision in key locations, such as the locker room or team website, to reinforce their importance.

Integrate the mission and vision into team discussions: Regularly refer to the mission and vision during team meetings, training sessions, and performance evaluations to ensure they remain top of mind.

Encourage player buy-in: Invite team members to share their thoughts on the mission and vision and discuss how they can contribute to their realization.

Recognize and celebrate progress: Acknowledge and reward team members who embody the mission and vision, reinforcing their importance and motivating others to do the same.

IV. Implementing the Team Mission and Vision

Transforming the mission and vision into tangible results requires consistent action and commitment from all team members. Here are some recommendations for successful implementation:

Align actions with the mission and vision: Ensure all team decisions, actions, and strategies are in line with the established mission and vision.

Develop a culture of accountability: Encourage team members to hold themselves and their teammates accountable for their contributions to the mission and vision, fostering a sense of ownership and responsibility among players.

Monitor progress and adjust as needed: Regularly review the team's progress towards its goals and adjust as necessary to stay on track. This may involve revisiting the mission and vision, revising strategies, or setting new goals.

Provide support and resources: Equip players and coaches with the necessary tools, resources, and training to effectively contribute to the team's mission and vision. This may include skill development programs, team-building activities, and opportunities for personal growth.

Foster a growth mindset: Encourage players to embrace challenges, learn from setbacks, and view obstacles as opportunities for growth. This mindset helps the team remain resilient and adaptive in the face of adversity, ultimately bringing them closer to realizing their mission and vision.

Conclusion

Developing a team mission and vision is a critical component of building a successful and cohesive hockey team. By creating a shared sense of purpose, direction, and identity, teams can unite their players and coaches under a common goal, fostering collaboration and determination.

Through effective communication and implementation of the mission and vision, hockey teams can drive performance, enhance player satisfaction, and establish a legacy of success.

CREATING A SUPPORTIVE AND INCLUSIVE ENVIRONMENT IN HOCKEY

A supportive and inclusive environment is fundamental to the success and well-being of all members within a hockey team. By fostering a sense of belonging, respect, and empathy, teams can maximize their potential and create an atmosphere in which players can thrive.

In this chapter, we will explore the importance of a supportive and inclusive environment in hockey, the challenges faced in achieving this goal, and the strategies and practices that can be employed to create a nurturing and diverse hockey community.

I. The Importance of a Supportive and Inclusive Environment in Hockey

Creating a supportive and inclusive environment in hockey is vital for the following reasons:

Player development: A positive atmosphere encourages individual growth and allows players to develop their skills, confidence, and resilience.

Team performance: An inclusive and supportive environment promotes collaboration, communication, and trust, which are essential for high-performing teams.

Player satisfaction: Players who feel valued, respected, and included are more likely to be committed and motivated to contribute to the team's success.

Attracting and retaining talent: A diverse and inclusive environment attracts a wider range of players and helps retain talented individuals who might otherwise leave due to feelings of exclusion or discomfort.

Social responsibility: Promoting inclusivity and support in hockey aligns with the broader social goal of combating discrimination and promoting equality.

II. Challenges to Creating a Supportive and Inclusive Environment

Despite the many benefits of a supportive and inclusive environment, various challenges can hinder its development:

Prejudice and discrimination: Stereotypes, biases, and discriminatory behavior can create barriers to inclusion and support within a team.

Lack of diversity: Homogeneity within a team can hinder the development of an inclusive environment, as players may be less exposed to different perspectives and experiences.

Resistance to change: Some individuals may be resistant to the adoption of new practices or the promotion of diversity and inclusion, impeding progress towards a supportive environment.

Limited resources and support: Teams may lack the necessary resources, knowledge, or support to create an inclusive and nurturing atmosphere.

III. Strategies for Creating a Supportive and Inclusive Environment

To overcome these challenges and cultivate a supportive and inclusive environment, hockey teams can employ the following strategies:
Develop an inclusive mission and vision: Establish a mission and vision that emphasizes the importance of diversity, inclusion, and support, and integrate these principles into the team's culture.

Encourage open communication: Foster an atmosphere in which players can express their thoughts, concerns, and experiences openly and without fear of judgment.

Provide education and training: Implement diversity and inclusion training programs to raise awareness of biases, stereotypes, and the importance of empathy and understanding.

Celebrate diversity: Highlight the unique backgrounds, experiences, and talents of each team member, and acknowledge the value that diversity brings to the team.

Establish a zero-tolerance policy: Implement a strict policy against discrimination, harassment, and bullying, and ensure that all team members are aware of the consequences of such behavior.

Promote accessibility: Implement measures to ensure that facilities, equipment, and activities are accessible to individuals with varying abilities, backgrounds, and needs.

IV. Best Practices for Fostering Inclusivity and Support

In addition to the strategies outlined above, the following best practices can help promote a supportive and inclusive environment in hockey:

1. Appoint a diversity and inclusion officer: Designate a team member or coach who is responsible for overseeing and promoting diversity and inclusion initiatives.

2. Encourage mentorship and peer support: Pair experienced players with newcomers or those who may feel isolated to provide guidance, encouragement, and friendship.

3. Provide resources and support: Offer resources, such as counseling services, mental health support, and educational materials, to help players navigate the challenges they may face in an inclusive environment.

4. Collaborate with external organizations: Partner with community organizations and advocacy groups that promote diversity, inclusion, and support in sports to learn from their expertise and broaden the team's network of resources.

5. Monitor progress and adjust as needed: Regularly assess the team's progress towards creating a supportive and inclusive environment and adjust as necessary to address any shortcomings or challenges that arise.

Here are five examples of this practice:

Hockey is for Everyone Initiative: The NHL's "Hockey is for Everyone" initiative aims to promote inclusiveness and diversity in the sport. The program focuses on providing opportunities for people of all backgrounds, regardless of race, color, religion, national origin, gender, disability, sexual orientation, and socio-economic status, to participate in hockey. The initiative also includes partnerships with organizations such as the You Can Play Project, which advocates for the inclusion of LGBTQ+ athletes in sports.

Women's Hockey Expansion: The growth of women's hockey has led to increased opportunities for female players and greater visibility for the sport. Organizations such as the Professional Women's Hockey Players Association (PWHPA) and the National Women's Hockey League (NWHL) have made strides in providing opportunities for female players to compete at a professional level. Furthermore, the inclusion of women's hockey in the Winter Olympics has showcased the talent and skill of female athletes on the global stage, inspiring a new generation of players.

The Ed Snider Youth Hockey Foundation: The Ed Snider Youth Hockey Foundation, established by the late Philadelphia Flyers owner Ed Snider, aims to provide underprivileged children in the Philadelphia area with opportunities to learn and play hockey. The foundation focuses on promoting life skills, academic achievement, and character development through on-ice and off-ice activities. By making hockey accessible to a diverse group of children, the foundation helps to break down barriers and create an inclusive environment within the sport.

Willie O'Ree's Legacy: Willie O'Ree, the first Black player in the NHL, has dedicated his life to promoting diversity and inclusiveness in hockey. As the NHL's Diversity Ambassador, O'Ree has worked tirelessly to engage with communities and provide opportunities for players from diverse backgrounds to participate in the sport. In recognition of his efforts, the NHL established the annual Willie O'Ree Community Hero Award, which honors individuals who have made significant contributions to diversity and inclusion within hockey.

Indigenous Hockey Programs: Various organizations and initiatives have been created to support the growth and development of hockey within Indigenous communities. Programs such as the Little Native Hockey League (LNHL) in Canada and the Native American Hockey Experience in the United States provide opportunities for Indigenous youth to participate in hockey, fostering cultural pride and inclusiveness within the sport. These programs aim to break down barriers and create an inclusive environment for Indigenous players, coaches, and fans.

Conclusion

Creating a supportive and inclusive environment in hockey is crucial for fostering player development, enhancing team performance, and promoting the well-being of all team members.

By implementing targeted strategies and best practices, teams can overcome challenges and cultivate an atmosphere in which players feel valued, respected, and included. Through this ongoing commitment to diversity, inclusion, and support, hockey teams can contribute to the broader goal of promoting equality and social responsibility within the sport and beyond.

ENCOURAGING OPEN COMMUNICATION AND FEEDBACK IN HOCKEY

Open communication and feedback play a critical role in the success and growth of a hockey team. By fostering a culture where team members feel comfortable expressing their thoughts, concerns, and ideas, teams can build trust, resolve conflicts, and drive improvement.

In this chapter, we will explore the importance of open communication and feedback in hockey, the barriers that may hinder effective communication, and strategies for promoting a culture of openness and constructive dialogue.

I. The Importance of Open Communication and

Feedback in Hockey

Open communication and feedback are vital to a hockey team for the following reasons:

Enhanced teamwork: Effective communication fosters collaboration, coordination, and teamwork, leading to improved performance on the ice.

Conflict resolution: Open dialogue allows for the expression and resolution of conflicts, helping to maintain a positive team atmosphere.

Learning and growth: Constructive feedback enables players and coaches to identify areas for improvement, set goals, and make necessary adjustments.

Trust and rapport: Open communication cultivates trust and rapport among team members, creating a strong foundation for collaboration and support.

Decision-making: Open dialogue enables the exchange of diverse perspectives and ideas, leading to more informed and effective decision-making.

II. Barriers to Open Communication and Feedback

Several factors can impede open communication and feedback within a hockey team:

Fear of criticism or rejection: Players and coaches may hesitate to express their thoughts or provide feedback due to concerns about negative reactions or damaging relationships.

Lack of trust: A lack of trust among team members can inhibit open communication and create an environment where individuals are reluctant to share their thoughts or concerns.

Inadequate communication skills: Team members may lack the necessary communication skills to effectively express their ideas, concerns, or feedback.

Hierarchical structures: Traditional hierarchical structures may deter open communication, as players may feel intimidated or unwilling to challenge those in positions of authority.

III. Strategies for Encouraging Open Communication and Feedback

To overcome these barriers and promote open communication and feedback, hockey teams can implement the following strategies:

Create a safe environment: Foster a team culture where individuals feel comfortable expressing their thoughts and concerns without fear of judgment, ridicule, or retribution.

Encourage active listening: Teach and model active listening skills, which involve fully focusing on the speaker, avoiding interruptions, and asking clarifying questions.

Provide constructive feedback: Offer feedback that is specific, timely, and actionable, focusing on behavior and performance rather than personal attributes.

Develop communication skills: Provide resources and training to help team members develop effective communication skills, such as assertiveness, empathy, and conflict resolution.

Encourage diverse perspectives: Promote the sharing of diverse viewpoints and experiences, emphasizing the value of different perspectives in enhancing decision-making and problem-solving.

IV. Best Practices for Fostering Open Communication and Feedback

In addition to the strategies outlined above, the following best practices can help create an environment that encourages open communication and feedback:

Establish regular team meetings: Schedule consistent team meetings to provide a forum for discussing progress, addressing concerns, and sharing feedback.

Implement an open-door policy: Encourage coaches and team leaders to maintain an open-door policy, signaling their availability and willingness to engage in open communication.

Use communication technology: Leverage technology, such as messaging apps and video conferencing tools, to facilitate communication and collaboration among team members.

Recognize and reward open communication: Acknowledge and celebrate instances of effective communication and feedback, reinforcing their importance and motivating others to engage in similar behavior.

Create opportunities for informal communication: Encourage casual conversations and social interactions among team members, which can help build rapport and trust.

Encouraging open communication and feedback in hockey is essential for fostering teamwork, promoting growth, and maintaining a positive team atmosphere.

By implementing targeted strategies and best practices, teams can overcome the barriers to effective communication and create an environment in which players and coaches feel comfortable expressing their thoughts and concerns.

Through this ongoing commitment to open dialogue and constructive feedback, hockey teams can build trust, enhance decision-making, and ultimately drive performance both on and off the ice.

PROMOTING MENTAL AND PHYSICAL WELL-BEING IN HOCKEY

The mental and physical well-being of players is paramount to the success and sustainability of a hockey team. By prioritizing the health of its players, a team can foster resilience, enhance performance, and prevent burnout.

In this chapter, we will explore the importance of mental and physical well-being in hockey, the challenges faced in maintaining a healthy balance, and strategies for promoting holistic wellness among players and coaches.

I. The Importance of Mental and Physical Well-Being in Hockey

Mental and physical well-being are crucial to a hockey team for the following reasons:

Enhanced performance: Players who are mentally and physically healthy can perform at their peak, contributing to the overall success of the team. Injury prevention: A focus on well-being helps prevent injuries by encouraging proper training, recovery, and self-care practices.

Longevity: Ensuring the mental and physical health of players promotes career longevity and reduces the risk of burnout.

Team culture: A team that prioritizes well-being fosters a positive and supportive environment where players feel valued and cared for.

Personal satisfaction: Players who maintain their mental and physical health are more likely to enjoy their hockey experience and develop a lifelong passion for the sport.

II. Challenges to Mental and Physical Well-Being in Hockey

Hockey players face various challenges that can impact their mental and physical well-being:

Intense physical demands: The fast-paced and physically demanding nature of hockey can lead to injuries, fatigue, and chronic pain.

Mental stress: High levels of competition, performance expectations, and pressure to succeed can contribute to stress, anxiety, and depression.

Balancing multiple roles: Many players juggle the demands of their hockey careers with personal, family, and academic responsibilities, potentially causing stress and burnout.

Limited access to resources: Players may lack access to adequate support services, such as mental health counseling or specialized medical care, which can hinder their ability to maintain their well-being.

III. Strategies for Promoting Mental and Physical Well-Being in Hockey

To address these challenges and prioritize the mental and physical well-being of players, hockey teams can implement the following strategies:

Establish a culture of well-being: Develop a team culture that values and emphasizes the importance of mental and physical health and integrates well-being practices into the team's routine.

Offer comprehensive support services: Provide access to a range of support services, including mental health counseling, sports medicine, nutrition, and strength and conditioning programs.

Encourage proper rest and recovery: Prioritize and schedule adequate rest and recovery time to allow players to recuperate and prevent injuries.

Promote stress management techniques: Teach and encourage the use of stress management techniques, such as mindfulness, meditation, and deep breathing exercises.

Foster open communication: Create an environment where players feel comfortable discussing their mental and physical health concerns and seeking support from coaches and teammates.

IV. Best Practices for Nurturing Mental and Physical Well-Being

In addition to the strategies outlined above, the following best practices can help promote mental and physical well-being in hockey:

1. Monitor player workload: Track and manage player workloads to prevent overtraining and ensure that players receive adequate rest and recovery.

2. Implement injury prevention programs: Develop and implement evidence-based injury prevention programs that focus on proper training techniques, strength and conditioning, and sport-specific skills.

3. Encourage a balanced lifestyle: Support players in maintaining a balanced lifestyle that includes time for personal, family, and academic commitments, as well as hobbies and interests outside of hockey.

4. Provide education on nutrition and hydration: Educate players on the importance of proper nutrition and hydration and provide guidance on optimal dietary practices to support performance and overall health.

5. Foster social connections: Encourage team bonding and the development of strong social connections among players, which can provide support and help alleviate stress.

6. Collaborate with professionals: Work with sports psychologists, physicians, nutritionists, and other professionals to

create a comprehensive approach to player well-being.

7. Address mental health stigma: Raise awareness about mental health issues and work to reduce stigma by promoting open dialogue and understanding.

Conclusion

Promoting mental and physical well-being in hockey is essential for ensuring the success, sustainability, and overall satisfaction of players and coaches.

By implementing targeted strategies and best practices, teams can address the challenges associated with maintaining a healthy balance in the demanding world of hockey. Through a commitment to holistic wellness, hockey teams can foster a positive and supportive environment that empowers players to thrive both on and off the ice.

DEVELOPING POSITIVE LEADERSHIP SKILLS: EMOTIONAL INTELLIGENCE

Emotional intelligence (EI) is a key component of effective leadership in the world of hockey. It encompasses the ability to recognize, understand, and manage one's emotions and the emotions of others, which is critical to building strong relationships, fostering team cohesion, and facilitating effective communication.

In this chapter, we will explore the importance of emotional intelligence in hockey leadership, the components of EI, and strategies for developing and enhancing these skills among coaches and team leaders.

I. The Importance of Emotional Intelligence in Hockey Leadership

Emotional intelligence is vital to hockey leadership for the following reasons:

1. Relationship-building: EI enables leaders to connect with their players on a deeper level, fostering trust, respect, and loyalty.

2. Team cohesion: Emotional intelligence helps leaders create a supportive and inclusive environment, promoting unity and collaboration among team members.

3. Effective communication: EI allows leaders to communicate more effectively by understanding and empathizing with the emotional needs and perspectives of their players.

4. Conflict resolution: Emotionally intelligent leaders can identify, address, and resolve

conflicts in a constructive manner, helping to maintain a positive team atmosphere.

5. Decision-making: EI enhances decision-making by considering the emotional and interpersonal aspects of various options and their potential impacts on the team.

II. Components of Emotional Intelligence

Emotional intelligence consists of four primary components:

Self-awareness: The ability to recognize and understand one's emotions, strengths, weaknesses, and their impact on others.

Self-management: The ability to regulate one's emotions, maintain composure, and adapt to changing circumstances.

Social awareness: The ability to empathize with others, recognize their emotions, and understand their perspectives.

Relationship management: The ability to develop and maintain strong relationships, communicate effectively, and resolve conflicts.

III. Strategies for Developing Emotional Intelligence in Hockey Leadership

To cultivate emotional intelligence among hockey leaders, the following strategies can be employed:

Practice self-reflection: Encourage leaders to engage in regular self-reflection, assessing their emotional responses, strengths, and areas for growth.

Seek feedback: Encourage leaders to seek feedback from players, coaches, and peers to gain insight into their emotional intelligence and areas for improvement.

Foster empathy: Teach and model empathy, encouraging leaders to put themselves in the shoes of their players and understand their emotions and perspectives.

Develop active listening skills: Train leaders to listen attentively, avoid interrupting, and ask clarifying questions to demonstrate understanding and empathy.

Engage in emotional regulation exercises: Provide leaders with tools and techniques for managing their emotions, such as deep breathing, mindfulness, and visualization.

Participate in EI training programs: Encourage leaders to attend workshops, seminars, or courses focused on developing emotional intelligence.

IV. Best Practices for Enhancing Emotional Intelligence in Hockey Leadership

In addition to the strategies outlined above, the following best practices can help hockey leaders develop and enhance their emotional intelligence:

Set an example: Model emotional intelligence by demonstrating empathy, active listening, and effective communication in your interactions with players and coaches.

Provide resources: Offer books, articles, and other resources related to emotional intelligence to help leaders deepen their understanding of the concept and its applications.

Encourage collaboration: Foster collaboration among team members, which can enhance social awareness and relationship management skills.

Recognize and reward EI development: Acknowledge and celebrate improvements in emotional intelligence, reinforcing the importance of these skills and motivating continued growth.

Foster a supportive environment: Create an atmosphere where leaders feel comfortable discussing their emotions and seeking guidance on developing their emotional intelligence.

Conclusion

Developing emotional intelligence in hockey leadership is crucial for building strong relationships, fostering team cohesion, and facilitating effective communication.

By implementing targeted strategies and best practices, coaches and team leaders can cultivate and enhance their EI skills, ultimately contributing to the overall success and well-being of their players and the team.

Emotionally intelligent leaders are better equipped to navigate the complexities and challenges of the hockey world, making a positive and lasting impact on their teams and the sport.

EFFECTIVE COMMUNICATION IN HOCKEY LEADERSHIP

Effective communication is a cornerstone of successful leadership in the world of hockey. It enables coaches and team leaders to convey their expectations, provide feedback, and foster collaboration among players, ultimately contributing to the overall success and performance of the team.

In this chapter, we will explore the importance of effective communication in hockey leadership, the components of effective communication, and strategies for developing and enhancing communication skills among coaches and team leaders.

I. The Importance of Effective Communication in Hockey Leadership

Effective communication is essential to hockey leadership for the following reasons:

1. Clarity of expectations: Clear communication allows coaches and leaders to convey their expectations to players, ensuring everyone is on the same page regarding goals, roles, and responsibilities.

2. Improved performance: Effective communication enables leaders to provide constructive feedback and guidance, helping players improve their skills and performance on the ice.

3. Enhanced teamwork: Strong communication skills facilitate collaboration and coordination among players, fostering a unified and cohesive team.

4. Conflict resolution: Effective communication is crucial for addressing and resolving

conflicts in a constructive manner, maintaining a positive team atmosphere.

5. Decision-making: Clear communication allows leaders to convey their rationale for decisions and gather input from players and staff, promoting transparency and buy-in.

II. Components of Effective Communication

Effective communication in hockey leadership involves several key components:

1. Verbal communication: The ability to articulate thoughts, expectations, and feedback clearly and concisely through spoken language.

2. Non-verbal communication: The ability to convey meaning through body language, facial expressions, gestures, and tone of voice.

3. Active listening: The ability to fully focus on the speaker, avoid interruptions, and ask clarifying questions to demonstrate understanding and empathy.

4. Adaptability: The ability to adjust communication styles and techniques based on the audience, context, and desired outcome.

5. Emotional intelligence: The ability to recognize, understand, and manage one's emotions and the emotions of others, facilitating effective communication and relationship-building.

III. Strategies for Developing Effective Communication in Hockey Leadership

To cultivate effective communication skills among hockey leaders, the following strategies can be employed:

1. Encourage self-assessment: Prompt leaders to reflect on their communication strengths and areas for improvement, setting goals for growth and development.

2. Provide feedback: Offer constructive feedback on leaders' communication skills, highlighting areas of success and opportunities for growth.

3. Teach active listening: Train leaders in active listening techniques, emphasizing the importance of giving their full attention, avoiding interruptions, and asking clarifying questions.

4. Foster adaptability: Encourage leaders to practice adapting their communication styles based on the audience, context, and desired outcome.

5. Leverage emotional intelligence: Emphasize the importance of emotional intelligence in effective communication, helping leaders

develop their empathy, self-awareness, and self-management skills.

IV. Best Practices for Enhancing Effective Communication in Hockey Leadership
In addition to the strategies outlined above, the following best practices can help hockey leaders develop and enhance their communication skills:

1. Model effective communication: Demonstrate strong communication skills in your interactions with players, coaches, and staff, setting a positive example for others to follow.

2. Offer resources and training: Provide access to resources and training opportunities focused on communication skills, such as books, articles, workshops, and courses.

3. Encourage open dialogue: Foster an environment where leaders feel comfortable discussing their communication challenges and seeking guidance from their peers and mentors.

4. Provide opportunities for practice: Create opportunities for leaders to practice their communication skills in various settings, such as team meetings, one-on-one conversations, and public speaking engagements.

5. Recognize and reward growth: Acknowledge and celebrate improvements in communication skills, reinforcing their importance and motivating continued development.

Effective communication is a critical aspect of successful leadership in the world of hockey. By implementing targeted strategies and best practices, coaches and team leaders can develop and enhance their communication skills, ultimately contributing to the overall success and performance of their players and the team.

Through clear communication, active listening, and adaptability, hockey leaders can foster a positive and cohesive team environment, enabling players to thrive both on and off the ice.

Here are three examples of strong communicators in the history of hockey:

Jean Béliveau: Widely regarded as one of the greatest hockey players of all time, Jean Béliveau was also known for his exceptional communication skills. As the captain of the Montreal Canadiens for a decade, Béliveau was respected for his ability to connect with his teammates, coaches, and fans. His calm demeanor, empathy, and eloquence made him an exemplary leader on and off the ice.

Wayne Gretzky: "The Great One" is not only famous for his unparalleled playing abilities but also for his strong communication skills. Throughout his career, Gretzky was known for his approachability, humility, and ability to relate to his teammates. As a captain and later as a coach, he was known for his ability to articulate his thoughts clearly, listen attentively to others, and inspire those around him to strive for greatness.

Brendan Shanahan: As a player, Brendan Shanahan was known for his leadership and communication skills, which contributed to his success as a leader for championship teams.

After retiring as a player, Shanahan took on various executive roles within the NHL, including the position of President and Alternate Governor of the Toronto Maple Leafs. In these roles, Shanahan has continued to demonstrate strong communication abilities, fostering a culture of openness, collaboration, and accountability within the organizations he leads.

CONFLICT RESOLUTION IN HOCKEY LEADERSHIP

Conflict is an inevitable part of any team sport, including hockey. Differences in opinions, values, and personalities can sometimes lead to friction among players, coaches, and staff members.

Effective conflict resolution is a crucial aspect of hockey leadership, as it enables teams to address and overcome these challenges in a constructive manner.

In this chapter, we will explore the importance of conflict resolution in hockey leadership, the types of conflicts that may arise, and strategies for resolving conflicts in a healthy and productive way.

I. The Importance of Conflict Resolution in Hockey Leadership

Conflict resolution is essential to hockey leadership for the following reasons:

Team cohesion: Resolving conflicts effectively helps maintain unity and cohesion among team members, fostering a supportive and collaborative environment.

Performance: By addressing and resolving conflicts in a timely manner, leaders can prevent distractions and negative emotions from impacting the team's performance on the ice.

Emotional well-being: Effective conflict resolution promotes the emotional well-being of players, coaches, and staff members by preventing prolonged stress and resentment.

Personal growth: Conflict can serve as an opportunity for growth and learning when approached constructively, helping individuals develop new skills and insights.

Reputation: A hockey team that effectively manages conflicts is likely to earn the respect of its peers, opponents, and fans, contributing to a positive reputation both on and off the ice.

II. Types of Conflicts in Hockey

Conflicts in hockey can arise from various sources, including:

Role ambiguity: Disagreements may occur when players, coaches, or staff members are unclear about their roles and responsibilities within the team. Personal differences: Conflicts can stem from differences in personalities, values, communication styles, or backgrounds among team members.

Performance issues: Disputes may arise when players or coaches perceive that certain individuals are not performing up to expectations or are receiving preferential treatment.

Resource allocation: Conflicts can occur when there are disagreements over the distribution of resources, such as ice time, equipment, or funding.

Decision-making: Disagreements may arise when team members have differing opinions on strategic decisions, coaching techniques, or player development.

III. Strategies for Conflict Resolution in Hockey Leadership

To effectively resolve conflicts among hockey players, coaches, and staff members, the following strategies can be employed:

Identify the root cause: Begin by identifying the underlying cause of the conflict, which may involve role ambiguity, personal differences, performance issues, resource allocation, or decision-making.

Encourage open communication: Facilitate open and honest communication among the involved parties, allowing everyone to express their thoughts, feelings, and concerns in a respectful manner.

Practice active listening: Encourage all parties to practice active listening, focusing on understanding and empathizing with the perspectives of others.

Maintain neutrality: As a leader, strive to remain neutral and objective during conflict resolution, avoiding any appearance of favoritism or bias.

Seek win-win solutions: Aim to find resolutions that address the needs and concerns of all parties involved, fostering a sense of collaboration and mutual satisfaction.

Establish clear expectations: Clarify roles, responsibilities, and expectations to prevent future conflicts stemming from role ambiguity.
Foster personal growth: Use conflicts as opportunities for personal growth and learning, encouraging individuals to develop new skills, insights, and understanding.

IV. Best Practices for Conflict Resolution in Hockey Leadership

In addition to the strategies outlined above, the following best practices can help hockey leaders effectively address and resolve conflicts:

1. Lead by example: Model effective conflict resolution skills in your own interactions with players, coaches, and staff members, setting a positive example for others to follow.

2. Prioritize timely resolution: Address conflicts promptly, preventing them from escalating and causing further harm to team cohesion and performance.

3. Provide training: Offer training and resources on conflict resolution to help players, coaches, and staff members develop the necessary skills and techniques for managing disagreements constructively.

4. Create a supportive environment: Foster a team culture that values open communication, empathy, and mutual respect, making it easier for individuals to address and resolve conflicts.

5. Encourage self-reflection: Prompt individuals involved in conflicts to engage in self-reflection, considering their role in the disagreement and potential areas for growth.

6. Monitor progress: Keep an eye on the resolution process and its aftermath, ensuring that the agreed-upon solutions are implemented and that any lingering issues are addressed.

Conclusion

Conflict resolution is a critical aspect of successful leadership in the world of hockey. By implementing targeted strategies and best practices, coaches and team leaders can effectively address and resolve conflicts among players, coaches, and staff members, ultimately contributing to the overall success and well-being of the team.

By fostering a culture of open communication, empathy, and collaboration, hockey leaders can create a positive and supportive environment where individuals can thrive both on and off the ice.

Here are three examples of a successful conflict resolution in the history of hockey:

The Gretzky-Messier Partnership: During their time with the Edmonton Oilers, Wayne Gretzky and Mark Messier became two of the greatest players in NHL history. Despite their differing leadership styles – Gretzky being more soft-spoken and diplomatic, while Messier was more vocal and intense – they managed to complement each other and maintain a successful partnership. They used open communication and mutual respect to address any potential conflicts, which ultimately led to the team winning four Stanley Cups together in the 1980s.

The 2004-2005 NHL Lockout Resolution: The 2004-2005 NHL lockout was a labor dispute that resulted in the cancellation of the entire 2004-2005 season. The conflict arose due to disagreements between the league's owners and players regarding salary caps, revenue sharing, and other financial matters. After months of intense negotiations and a willingness to compromise, both parties eventually reached an agreement in July 2005, which resulted in the implementation of a new Collective Bargaining Agreement (CBA). This agreement addressed the concerns of both parties and led to the resumption of the NHL for the 2005-2006 season.

The Patrick Roy Trade: In December 1995, Patrick Roy, one of the greatest goaltenders in NHL history, demanded a trade from the Montreal Canadiens following a public falling-out with then-head coach Mario Tremblay. The conflict between Roy and Tremblay had been brewing for some time, with tensions coming to a head when Tremblay left Roy in net for nine goals during a game against the

Detroit Red Wings. The Canadiens' management acted swiftly to address the situation, trading Roy to the Colorado Avalanche. This resolution allowed Roy to have a fresh start and ultimately led to continued success in his career, as he won two more Stanley Cups with the Avalanche. Additionally, the trade served as a wake-up call for the Canadiens' organization, highlighting the importance of effective communication and conflict resolution within a team.

DECISION-MAKING AND PROBLEM SOLVING IN HOCKEY LEADERSHIP

Decision-making and problem-solving are fundamental aspects of hockey leadership, as coaches and team leaders are regularly faced with choices that can impact the team's performance, dynamics, and overall success.

In this chapter, we will explore the importance of effective decision-making and problem-solving in hockey leadership, the various decision-making models, and strategies for honing these crucial leadership skills.

I. The Importance of Decision-Making and Problem Solving in Hockey Leadership

Effective decision-making and problem-solving are essential to hockey leadership for the following reasons:

Performance: The decisions made by coaches and leaders can directly impact the team's performance, from the selection of players and allocation of ice time to the implementation of game strategies and adjustments.

Team dynamics: Decisions related to team culture, communication, and conflict resolution can significantly influence the dynamics and cohesion within the team.

Resource management: Leaders must make informed decisions about the allocation of resources, such as budgeting, equipment, and facilities, to support the team's success.

Player development: Decisions made by coaches and leaders can shape the growth and development of individual players, both on and off the ice.

Reputation: The choices made by hockey leaders can impact the team's reputation within the hockey community, affecting relationships with fans, opponents, and potential recruits.

II. Decision-Making Models in Hockey Leadership

Various decision-making models can be employed by hockey leaders, depending on the context and specific needs of the team:

Rational decision-making: This model involves a structured, step-by-step approach, where leaders identify objectives, gather, and evaluate relevant information, and choose the most logical option based on a thorough analysis of the alternatives.

Intuitive decision-making: This model relies on leaders' intuition, experience, and gut feelings, often allowing them to make quick decisions in situations where information may be limited or time sensitive.

Collaborative decision-making: This model involves seeking input and feedback from players, assistant coaches, and staff members, fostering a more inclusive and democratic decision-making process.

Data-driven decision-making: In this model, leaders use quantitative data and analytics to inform their choices, helping to minimize biases and enhance objectivity.

III. Strategies for Improving Decision-Making and Problem-Solving Skills in Hockey Leadership

To develop and enhance decision-making and problem-solving skills among hockey leaders, the following strategies can be employed:

Encourage self-assessment: Prompt leaders to reflect on their decision-making strengths and areas for improvement, setting goals for growth and development.

Provide training and resources: Offer access to training opportunities, workshops, and resources focused on decision-making and problem-solving skills.

Foster critical thinking: Encourage leaders to think critically and analytically about the choices they face, considering potential consequences, risks, and benefits.

Promote adaptability: Help leaders develop the ability to adapt their decision-making approach based on the context and specific needs of the team.

Practice scenario-based learning: Use real-life or hypothetical scenarios to help leaders practice their decision-making and problem-solving skills in a safe and supportive environment.

IV. Best Practices for Decision-Making and Problem Solving in Hockey Leadership

In addition to the strategies outlined above, the following best practices can help hockey leaders make effective decisions and solve problems:

1. Lead by example: Model strong decision-making and problem-solving skills in your own leadership role, setting a positive example for others to follow.

2. Embrace diverse perspectives: Encourage open dialogue and seek input from a diverse range of team members, recognizing the value of different perspectives and experiences.

3. Maintain an open mind: Be willing to reevaluate decisions and adjust course as needed, demonstrating flexibility and adapt ability in the face of changing circumstances.

4. Balance speed and accuracy: Strive to balance the need for timely decision-making with the importance of making well-informed and

accurate choices, considering the potential consequences and risks involved.

5. Communicate effectively: Clearly communicate the rationale behind decisions to players, coaches, and staff members, helping to build trust and understanding within the team.

6. Learn from experience: Reflect on past decisions and problem-solving experiences, identifying lessons learned and opportunities for growth and development.

7. Establish a decision-making framework: Develop a consistent framework for decision-making within the team, outlining the processes, criteria, and values that should guide choices and actions.

Conclusion

Decision-making and problem-solving are critical aspects of successful leadership in the world of hockey. By implementing targeted strategies and best practices, coaches and team leaders can develop and enhance their decision-making and problem-solving skills, ultimately contributing to the overall success and performance of their players and the team.

Through a combination of rational, intuitive, collaborative, and data-driven approaches, hockey leaders can make well-informed choices and effectively address the challenges they face, fostering a positive and successful team environment both on and off the ice.

INSPIRING PEAK PERFORMANCE IN HOCKEY LEADERSHIP

Inspiring peak performance is a key objective for hockey leaders, as it contributes to the overall success of the team, individual players, and the organization.

In this chapter, we will explore the importance of inspiring peak performance in hockey leadership, the factors that contribute to peak performance, and strategies for motivating and inspiring players and staff to reach their full potential.

I. The Importance of Inspiring Peak Performance in Hockey Leadership

Inspiring peak performance in hockey leadership is vital for the following reasons:

Team success: A team that consistently performs at its best is more likely to achieve its goals, from winning games and championships to fostering a positive and supportive team culture.

Player development: Encouraging players to reach their full potential supports their growth and development, both on and off the ice.

Motivation: Inspiring peak performance fosters a sense of motivation, commitment, and pride among players, coaches, and staff members.

Reputation: A team that demonstrates consistent high performance is more likely to attract the attention of fans, sponsors, and potential recruits, enhancing the organization's reputation.

Personal satisfaction: Hockey leaders who successfully inspire peak performance can experience a sense of personal satisfaction and achievement, knowing that they have made a positive impact on their team.

II. Factors Contributing to Peak Performance

Several factors can contribute to peak performance in hockey, including:

Physical fitness: Ensuring that players are in top physical condition, through strength training, conditioning, and proper nutrition, is crucial for optimal performance.

Mental preparedness: Mental skills, such as focus, confidence, and resilience, play a significant role in peak performance.

Technical skills: Mastering the technical aspects of the game, including skating, shooting, and puck handling, is essential for high-level performance.

Tactical knowledge: A deep understanding of game strategies, systems, and opponents can enhance a team's ability to perform at its best.

Team cohesion: A strong sense of unity, trust, and support among team members can contribute to collective peak performance.

III. Strategies for Inspiring Peak Performance in Hockey Leadership

To inspire peak performance in hockey players and staff, leaders can employ the following strategies:

Set high expectations: Clearly communicate your expectations for performance and effort, emphasizing the importance of striving for excellence in all aspects of the game.

Foster a growth mindset: Encourage players and staff to view challenges as opportunities for growth and learning, rather than as obstacles or setbacks.

Provide constructive feedback: Offer regular, specific, and actionable feedback to help individuals identify areas for improvement and develop the necessary skills to perform at their best.

Celebrate success: Recognize and celebrate individual and team achievements, reinforcing the importance of hard work and dedication in reaching peak performance.

Promote mental skills training: Encourage the development of mental skills, such as goal setting, visualization, and relaxation techniques, to support optimal performance.

Encourage teamwork: Foster a culture of collaboration, trust, and support, emphasizing the importance of working together to achieve common goals.

Be a role model: Demonstrate commitment to peak performance in your own actions, setting an example for players and staff to follow.

IV. Best Practices for Inspiring Peak Performance in Hockey Leadership

In addition to the strategies outlined above, the following best practices can help hockey leaders inspire peak performance:

Maintain open communication: Encourage open and honest communication, allowing players and staff to express their thoughts, concerns, and ideas.

Tailor your approach: Recognize that individuals have different motivations and respond to different types of encouragement; tailor your approach to best suit the needs of each player and staff member.

Develop individualized plans: Work with each player and staff member to create personalized plans for growth and development, considering their unique strengths, weaknesses, and goals.

Create a supportive environment: Foster a positive and inclusive team culture that promotes learning, growth, and mutual support, enabling individuals to feel comfortable taking risks and pushing their boundaries.

Prioritize physical and mental well-being: Ensure that players and staff have access to resources and support for maintaining their physical and mental health, recognizing that well-being is a crucial component of peak performance.

Encourage continuous learning: Promote a culture of lifelong learning and improvement, emphasizing the importance of staying up to date with the latest techniques, strategies, and developments in the hockey world.

Evaluate progress and adjust strategies: Regularly assess the effectiveness of your efforts to inspire peak performance, adjusting your approach as needed to ensure continued success.

Conclusion

Inspiring peak performance is an essential aspect of hockey leadership, as it contributes to the overall success and development of players, coaches, and staff members.

By implementing targeted strategies and best practices, hockey leaders can effectively motivate and inspire their teams to reach their full potential, both on and off the ice.

Through a combination of high expectations, individualized support, mental skills training, and a strong focus on teamwork, hockey leaders can create an environment where peak performance becomes the norm, fostering a culture of excellence, growth, and achievement.

Here are five examples of lesser-known stories of players hitting peak performance using these techniques:

1. Angela James: As one of the first women to break into professional hockey, Angela James was a trailblazer for women's hockey in Canada. She was known for her exceptional leadership skills, leading by example with her dedication and work ethic. James helped lead the Canadian women's hockey team to four world championships and was the first woman to be inducted into the Hockey Hall of Fame.

2. Rick Tocchet: A former NHL player and current coach, Rick Tocchet was known for

his positive leadership style during his playing career. He was a vocal leader on and off the ice, known for his ability to motivate his teammates and build a positive team culture. Tocchet played a key role in helping the Pittsburgh Penguins win the Stanley Cup in 1992.

3. Willie Mitchell: A former NHL defenseman, Willie Mitchell was known for his leadership both on and off the ice. He was a vocal presence in the locker room, known for his ability to motivate his teammates and build a positive team culture. Mitchell helped lead the Los Angeles Kings to two Stanley Cup championships in 2012 and 2014.

4. Hayley Wickenheiser: A Canadian hockey player and Olympic gold medalist, Hayley Wickenheiser was known for her exceptional leadership skills on and off the ice. She was a vocal leader in the locker room, known for her ability to motivate and inspire her

teammates. Wickenheiser played a key role in leading the Canadian women's hockey team to four Olympic gold medals and seven world championships.

5. Georges Laraque: A former NHL player and current commentator, Georges Laraque was known for his positive leadership style during his playing career. He was a vocal leader on and off the ice, known for his ability to build a positive team culture and motivate his teammates. Laraque played a key role in helping the Edmonton Oilers reach the Stanley Cup finals in 2006.

THE LONG-TERM IMPACT OF POSITIVE LEADERSHIP ON TEAMS AND ORGANIZATIONS

Positive leadership is becoming an increasingly important aspect of successful teams and organizations in the world of hockey. As sport continues to evolve and becomes more competitive, the need for effective leadership and strong team cultures has never been greater. Here are some potential long-term future outlooks for positive leadership in the world of hockey:

Increased emphasis on diversity, equity, and inclusion: With a growing recognition of the importance of diversity and inclusiveness within the sport, hockey organizations are likely to place a greater emphasis on positive leadership practices that foster a sense of belonging and respect among all players, coaches, and staff members. Teams that prioritize DEI initiatives and practices are likely to attract a wider range of talented players and staff, contributing to the overall success of the organization.

Continued focus on mental health and well-being: As the mental and physical demands of playing professional hockey continue to be a challenge for players, positive leadership practices that prioritize mental health and well-being are likely to become even more important. Teams that provide resources and support for their players and staff to maintain optimal mental and physical health are likely to have a competitive advantage in attracting and retaining top talent.

Integration of technology and data-driven decision-making: As technology continues to play an increasingly important role in sports, the use of data-driven decision-making and performance analysis is likely to become even more prevalent in the world of hockey. Positive leadership that can effectively incorporate technology and data into their decision-making processes will be better positioned to achieve success on and off ice.

Increased focus on leadership development: As the importance of positive leadership in hockey becomes more widely recognized, there may be a greater emphasis on leadership development programs for coaches and team leaders.

Programs that focus on the development of leadership skills such as emotional intelligence, communication, conflict resolution, and decision-making can help to foster a culture of positivity and success within teams and organizations.

Overall, the outlook for positive leadership in the world of hockey looks bright. As teams and organizations continue to recognize the importance of fostering a positive and supportive team culture, the implementation of effective leadership practices will become even more essential for achieving long-term success on and off ice.